# Worrying Too Much

## Learning How to Manage Stress

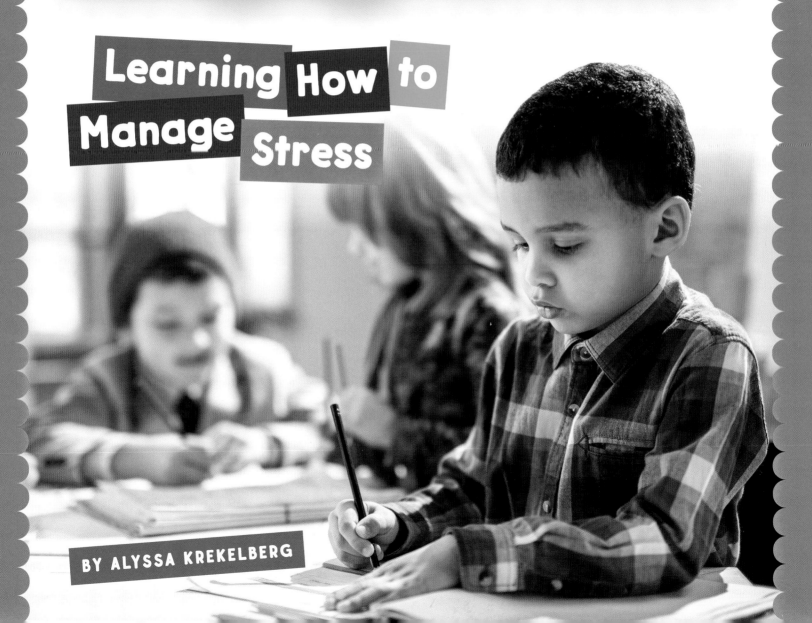

BY ALYSSA KREKELBERG

**The Child's World®**

**childsworld.com**

Published by The Child's World®
1980 Lookout Drive • Mankato, MN 56003-1705
800-599-READ • www.childsworld.com

Photographs ©: iStockphoto, cover, 1, 10,
13, 14, 21; SDI Productions/iStockphoto,
5, 6, 9; Shutterstock Images, 17, 18

ISBN 9781503844537 (Reinforced Library Binding)
ISBN 9781503846746 (Portable Document Format)
ISBN 9781503847934 (Online Multi-user eBook)
LCCN 2019956653

Printed in the United States of America

## ABOUT THE AUTHOR

Alyssa Krekelberg is a
children's book editor
and author. She lives
in Minnesota with her
hyper husky.

# Contents

# CHAPTER ONE

# Talking about Stress

Emily's grandpa is in the hospital. It makes her sad. She has not been hungry. She does not talk much. And when she does talk, she is cranky.

Emily's mom notices that something is wrong. She asks if Emily is **stressed**.

When people you care about are sick, it can make you feel stressed.

You may feel better when other people feel the same way that you feel.

Emily listens to her mom explain being stressed. She is glad there is a name for this feeling she has.

Emily's mom says, "I also feel stressed. I am worried about grandpa."

"Sometimes, talking to people about your feelings will make you feel less stressed," Emily's mom says.

"I feel better after talking to you," Emily says. She does not feel upset. Emily is thankful that she has family members she can talk to about her feelings.

It is important to talk about your emotions with people you trust.

9

You may feel upset if you cannot find something you are looking for.

# CHAPTER TWO

# Dealing with Stress

Andy is working on a project for school. He uses a computer to look for information. But Andy cannot find the right information.

The teacher says that computer time is almost over. Andy's stomach hurts.

Andy frowns and stares at the screen. He feels stressed.

"Are you OK?" his friend Steven asks. "You look upset."

"I cannot find information," Andy says. "It is too **difficult**."

"Can I help you?" Steven asks. "We can look together."

It is important to find help if you are feeling stressed.

Getting rid of stress can make you feel better.

Andy nods. He and Steven look at different websites. They look for new **sources**. Andy and Steven find the information that Andy needs for his project.

Andy smiles and thanks Steven for the help. Then he starts writing the answers to his project. Andy is glad that his friend helped him feel less stressed.

# CHAPTER THREE

# Finding a Way to Cope

Nikki does not want to talk to anyone. Her stomach and head hurt. She feels angry and sad at the same time.

Nikki's parents are getting a **divorce**. "I feel very stressed," Nikki tells her mom.

Stress can make people feel sick.

Sometimes you might cry if you are stressed.

18

Nikki's mom understands. She tells Nikki that she is stressed, too. "You can always tell me about your feelings," her mom says.

**THINK ABOUT IT!**

**When was a time that you were stressed? How did you feel?**

**What is one way that you can avoid stress? If you cannot avoid it, what can you do to feel better?**

"I like to draw my feelings," Nikki's mom says.

Nikki draws. She likes seeing her emotions on paper. Nikki still feels stressed, but understanding her emotions helps her feel better.

Art is one way to deal with stress.

# GLOSSARY

**difficult** (DIH-fih-kult) Something difficult is hard. Andy had a difficult time finding information on the computer.

**divorce** (dih-VORSS) A divorce is when two married people decide not to be married anymore. Nikki felt stressed because of her parent's divorce.

**sources** (SOR-sez) Sources are places where you can find information. Andy and Steven looked for new sources.

**stressed** (STRESD) If someone feels a lot of emotional or mental pressure, he or she is stressed. Emily is stressed because her grandpa is sick.

# TO LEARN MORE

## Books

Dinmont, Kerry. *Sad.* Mankato, MN:
The Child's World, 2019.

DiOrio, Rana. *What Does It Mean to Be Present?*
Naperville, IL: Little Pickle Press, 2017.

Grossman, Laurie M. *Master of Mindfulness: How
to Be Your Own Superhero in Times of Stress.*
Oakland, CA: New Harbinger Publications, 2016.

## Websites

Visit our website for links about managing stress:
**childsworld.com/links**

*Note to Parents, Teachers, and Librarians: We routinely verify our Web links to make
sure they are safe and active sites. So encourage your readers to check them out!*

# INDEX